The Streets Don't Love You Back
Lifeskills
Intervention Program

The Streets Don't Love You Back Lifeskills Intervention Program

Author

Lucinda F. Boyd R.N.

"You can become anyone you want to be!
It doesn't matter what happened to you or what you've done!!
What matters is what you do next!"

Copyright

Copyright © 2015 Lucinda F. Boyd R.N.

First Printing: 2015

ISBN 978-1-5136-0346-9

THE STREETS DON'T LOVE YOU BACK
MISSION STATEMENT

It is our mission to be a force for positive change and inspire others to greatness.

We will trust our dreams and be the prisoner of nothing. We will strive to continually invent the future out of our imagination rather than be victims of the past.

We will live true to the principles of charity, honesty, integrity, courage, justice, humility, kindness, respect, loyalty to self, trust, knowledge, understanding and non-violence.

We will use our personal defeats and victories unselfishly to help enrich the lives of all who cross our path by caring and affirming their unique worth, by giving what we have to give and teaching them what we know.

We will strive to educate others about the dangers of gang violence and drug activity and that there are many alternatives to the gang, thug, drug, life.

We will encourage others to rise up and believe that they can be a greater person and believe that they can achieve whatever they want in life.

We will embrace and see each day as not just another day, but one filled with opportunity and excitement as we remember that the pursuit of happiness and excellence will determine the choices we make and the paths we choose to travel.

We choose to make a difference in this world.

Our movement is striving to educate the youth and others about the dangers of gangs, drugs, violence and abuse and that there are many alternatives to that life. That with the right tools you can make positive changes.

Our focus is educating through true stories of people who used to be involved in the gang, thug, drug, violent, abusive street life and how living/surviving the street life has affected their lives, the lives of others, how they have changed their life and what they are doing now.

Our goal is that, The Streets Don't Love You Back Radio Show, The Streets Don't Love You Back TV, our Speaking Engagements, our Life skills Intervention Program, our Ex-Offender Programs and our Mentoring Programs will be vehicle's to educate and make change. Rob and I believe that through our vision and The Streets Don't Love You Back Movement we can and will create change and healing for many people in our country. This is our Mission

Lucinda F. Boyd R.N.

Lucinda F. Boyd R.N. and Robert D. Boyd Jr.
Founders of The Streets Don't Love You Back Movement

Chapter One

Substance Abuse Dependency, Making Decisions

Substance Dependency is a Disease

Alcohol is such a big part of American life today that we rarely stop to consider our pattern of drinking. We drink wine with dinner, or have a few drinks after work, or even a few beers while watching a ball game, but when a pattern of drinking begins to emerge, it can become a problem.

Drug use in America is also more commonplace than it once was. In today's teenage population over 90 percent have used alcohol. Over 50 percent have used marijuana, 17 percent admit to trying cocaine and 12.5 percent have used some form of hallucinogen.

Why Do We Drink or Use Drugs?

Many people feel that it is necessary to drink or experiment with drugs when at parties and social gatherings.

Some people drink or abuse drugs as a way to cope with the daily stress and tension from school or work, or to cope with other problems such as marital distress or even physical illness.

Alcohol and drugs may become a substitute for satisfying personal relationships, challenging work or self-fulfillment.

Some may use alcohol and drugs as a way to compensate for feelings of guilt, shame, shyness or low self-esteem and loneliness.

When drinking or drug use becomes a means for coping with life's problems it can turn into addiction. Unfortunately alcohol and some drugs have become more socially acceptable, and this makes it even easier for people to experiment at younger ages. In addition, alcohol and drugs are readily accessible to many of today's youth, which further increases the likelihood that they will use substances at some time.

Did You Know?

The average age of first experimentation with drugs is 13 and for alcohol it is even younger. Drug use has been classified as a major problem for kids as early as fourth grade by the students themselves.

Alcohol is the most widely used drug in America. It is the third largest cause of death in the United States, second only to heart disease and cancer. Alcohol and tobacco use are a significant "risk factor" in heart disease and cancer. It accounts for over 100,000 deaths per year in this country alone. It is also the leading cause of death for people between the ages of 15 and 24.

Alcohol and other drugs contribute to over 50 percent of all suicides and over 50 percent of all violent crimes.

Over 60 percent of admissions to emergency rooms are either directly or indirectly due to drug or alcohol usage.

Over 50 percent of all traffic accidents involve the use of drugs or alcohol, with many of these being fatal.

It is estimated that drugs and alcohol are a factor in at least 80 percent of domestic violence incidents.

Alcohol and drug use contributes to 60 percent of all sub-standard job performance and at least 40 percent of all industrial accidents.

Alcohol and drug addiction are treatable. However, it is our most untreated disease in the United States. It is estimated that 35 out of 36 alcoholics never receive treatment of any kind. This number is increased significantly when drug addiction of all kinds is included.

More than 60 percent of college women who have contracted sexually transmitted diseases, herpes or AIDS were intoxicated at the time of infection.

28 percent of all college dropouts are alcohol users.

Individuals between the ages of 16 and 24 are involved in more than one-third of all alcohol related traffic accidents.

95 percent of all college campus violence is alcohol related.

More than 40 percent of all college students with academic problems are alcohol users.

Perceptions of Drug Abuse

The prevalence of material related to drug abuse on television, in the news media and in messages in communities has made drug abuse seem like a widespread epidemic, commonly associated with negative stereotypes. As a result, people who use drugs are frequently perceived as bad and dangerous or as outlaws. Sometimes the media portray drug abuse as "cool" and adventurous. Whether the portrayal is positive or negative, substance abuse is often seen as a free choice, and those who abuse drugs face harsh attitudes and prejudice from others who see them as weak and selfish enough to choose to abuse drugs.

Why do some people end up abusing drugs and other do not?

There are various risk factors that can affect young people, such as living in a neighborhood where drug dealing and drug abuse are taking place and where out of school activities are not available. Economic strain on families where parents struggle to meet living costs can influence family relationships negatively, while spending time with peers who are involved in drugs or delinquency while seeking adventure puts young people at higher risk of falling prey to drug abuse. As a consequence of these kinds of risk factors, young people may suffer from mental health problems, making them even more vulnerable to substance abuse. It is not so much the case that all young people freely choose to use drugs, as that these kinds of risk factors may influence young people to initiate substance abuse.

In the case of tobacco and alcohol, the industries spend a lot of money on subliminal advertising to get young people, especially in developing countries, to use their products. Being a youth is also a time for self-discovery and trying new things. Peers who experiment with drugs and talk about substance abuse may give the impression that everybody is doing it.

Many of the negative stereotypes that surround people who abuse drugs come from the way they are most often seen in public. Television and other media may portray people who abuse drugs as irrational and their unpredictable behavior frightening.

Heavy or dependent drugs users have often lost their job and/or home and lack many of the physical conditions needed for a healthy and productive lifestyle. The negative stereotypes, stigma and prejudice assigned to people who abuse drugs usually complicate the problem and make it difficult for those in need of treatment and social support to get help. People who abuse drugs are often cut off from their communities and relationships and often homeless and living on the streets.

A substance abuser may become unable to go to school or work as the drugs affect their brain, thinking, concentration and memory as well as their body. As a result of substance abuse and the way it affects the brain, thinking and memory and relationships with family, friends and community, people who abuse drugs are not able to be responsible persons in their communities or become successful mentors to young people. Getting past the incorrect and harmful stereotypes that society often assigns to people who abuse drugs, becomes apparent that drug abuse is often not a free choice or a moral question.

Vulnerability?

Many reasons are given in explanation of drug abuse among young people. Some say it is because teenagers want to seem "cool" or are pressured by their peers to fit into a social circle where drugs are abused. While this may be true, there are many other important factors that will influence a young person to start abusing drugs. A proper understanding of those factors is another important step towards reducing the stigma attached to drug abuse and preventing addiction among youth around the world.

Young people are influenced by a number of factors at any given time. A person's temperament or personality traits, factors such as the stability of their upbringing, family life and bonds with family members and factors related to school, such as positive involvement in school activities, as well as community factors, such as the degree of availability of illicit drugs, all influence young people's development, day-to-day lives, relationships with family, friends and peers and self-image.

Some individual, family and community factors can put young people more at risk and make them vulnerable to experimentation with drugs and eventual drug abuse and dependence. Examples of risk factors are having a specific temperament or particular personality traits, a family history of addiction, a family member who abuses drugs, negative relationships with parents that lack bonding and warmth, neglect and abuse, lack of a family or home, friends who experiment with or use drugs, living in a community where drug abuse is common and a lack of schooling or employment. Insufficient rest and nutrition may also put an individual at greater risk, so it is important to maintain a balanced diet and get enough sleep. The more risk factors that are present in a person's life, the more likely it is that he or she will start experimenting with or continue to abuse drugs in a regular pattern and eventually become dependent.

However, a young person might be exposed to all of these negative risk factors and still never try drugs, thanks to a number of protective factors that also exist at the individual, family and community levels. These might include, at the individual level, a good sense of discipline, healthy self-esteem, good problem-solving skills, good self-expression abilities, a good ability to recognize and communicate emotions, an ability to maintain mental well-being and to cope with stress or anxiety and an ability to establish personal goals. At the family level, strong, healthy parental bonding and consistent family rules, may help to protect family members from risky behavior. At the community level the protective factors include attending a school that has explicit policies on substance abuse and living in a safe and caring community that supports the well-being of its members. Sadly, once a person starts abusing drugs, the risk factors tend to outweigh the protective factors.

Risk factors such as poverty, the availability of drugs and alienation grow even stronger as a person becomes more dependent on drugs. The good news is that the protective factors can be strengthened if young people learn new and improve existing skills before they experiment with or start abusing drugs.

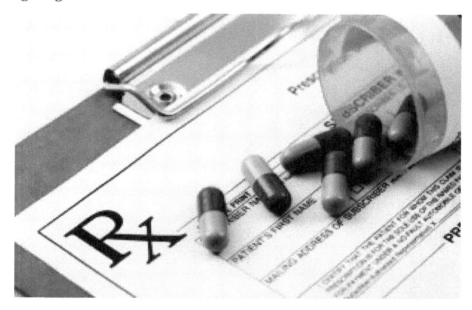

Abuse of prescription drugs

Many people, young and old, think that just because pharmaceutical drugs are used to treat medical conditions and diseases, that are prescribed by a doctor and come from a pharmacy, they are safer to take than illicit street drugs. However, prescription drugs function in similar ways to illegal Drugs, and if not taken as prescribed by a doctor, can have equally dangerous effects on the brain and body and can lead to an overdose, just like illicit drugs. Only trained medical doctors can prescribe drugs and they should be purchased only from licensed pharmacies where trained pharmacists can dispense and sell them.

Still, people decide to use prescription drugs for non-medical purposes, often for reasons similar to those associated with illicit drug use, or as an alternative to illicit drugs. Prescription drugs are often more easily available, for example in the family medicine cabinet, together with

15

information on ingredients, expected effects and dosages, making them seem safer than illicit drugs bought on the streets. Sometimes friends may share or sell medication that was prescribed for them. People often do not realize that sharing or selling prescription medication even with somebody who is in pain and seems to need medication is neither safe nor legal.

Some people, including young persons, use prescription drugs to self-medicate when they are feeling down or when they are in acute pain, using medication found in the family medicine cabinet. Self-medication is dangerous and can lead to dependence.

Young people may also try to enhance their abilities or performance by using prescription drugs, for example, to stay awake to study for exams. Again, prescription drugs should not be used for any purpose other than to treat medical conditions or in any way other than as prescribed by a medical doctor.

For all these reasons, it is important to raise awareness about prescription drug abuse, and to help prevent such abuse among young people.

Acute Physical Effects

Increased heart rate and skin temperature;

Impaired muscle control causing poor coordination, slurred speech, impaired motor skills;

Dizziness, vomiting, vision problems; and

Loss of consciousness, respiratory arrest and death.

Acute Effects on Mental Abilities

Judgment is frequently the first mental capacity affected by alcohol and drugs.

Poor decision making, rapid decision making, not being realistic in decisions is common;

Poor attention and concentration;

Loss of inhibitions-we say things or do things that we normally would not;

Exaggerated emotion (anger, fear, anxiety, sadness); and/or

Blackouts with loss of memory for events.

Long Terms Effects of Substance Use

Nutritional deficiencies effecting mental abilities;

Damage to physical organs including the brain, liver, heart, stomach;

Breakdown of bone and muscle tissue;

Memory loss or impairment;

Impaired attention and concentration;

Inability to get along with others;

Difficulty coping with school or employment demands; and/or

Alcohol withdrawal effects-tremors, excessive perspiration, hallucinations.

Do You Have a Drug or Alcohol Problem?

Denial is the main symptom of drug users and alcoholics. They deny that they really have a problem. This makes it more difficult for them to be realistic about the extent of their substance use, and to recognize that it may be a problem.

90% of addictions start in the teenage years

1 in 6 teens have used medicine to get high

27% of teens AND 16% of parents believe that using prescription drugs to get high is safer than using street drugs to get high

Test Yourself!

Have you ever felt like you should cut down on your drinking and/or drug use? Yes/ No

Have you ever felt irritated by criticism of your drinking and/or drug use? Yes/ No

Have you ever felt guilty about your drinking, drug use or your behavior during its use? Yes/ No

Do you ever take a drink or use drugs in the morning? Yes/ No

If you answered yes to one of these questions, the possibility that you are alcohol or drug dependent is significantly increased. This may also mean that although you are not dependent on drugs or alcohol at this time, you could become dependent if your pattern of abuse continues.

If you answered yes to two of these questions, it is very likely that you are dependent on drugs or alcohol.

If you answered yes to three or four of these questions, there is a greater than 95 percent chance that you are dependent on drugs or alcohol. Please seek assistance for your drug or alcohol problem immediately.

What is the Next Step?

If you think that you may have an alcohol or drug problem there are many sources of assistance that are available to you. For treatment or referral information:

Speak to a counselor, there are many different alternatives to outpatient treatment for substance abuse and dependence. Some available options include: individual counseling, group counseling and networking with other inpatient and day treatment programs in the local area. These options are all tailored to each individual's needs.

Call the local chapter of Alcoholics Anonymous, Narcotics Anonymous or Cocaine Anonymous. These numbers are all listed in the phone book.

Speak with your family doctor about your current level of drug or alcohol abuse, and request a referral to a treatment center or counselor that can help.

Speak with your church priest or church minister. Discuss the different options that may be available through your church for your substance abuse problems.

Substance Dependency and Addiction is a progressive disease. These problems do not normally improve on their own.

CHOOSE TO BE ALCOHOL AND DRUG FREE

MAKING GOOD DECISIONS

Decision making skills will help you make good choices. The choices you make will help you get where you want to go. Your decisions will allow you to shape your life. Developing effective decision making skills will help you get what you need and want.

All of us are confronted with various decisions to make on a daily basis. Some are small and of minor consequence, while others are huge and potentially life changing. Some are simple and obvious choices; others are more difficult and painstaking. For those that are complex and difficult to make, there is a process we can follow to help us come up with a good solution.

The Keys to Making a Good Decision

Identify the decision to be made as well as the objectives or outcome you want to achieve.

Do your homework. Gather as many facts and as much information you can to assess your options.

Brainstorm and come up with several possible choices. Determine if the options are compatible with your values, interests and abilities.

Weigh the probabilities or possible outcomes. In other words, what's the worst that can happen? What will happen if I do A, B or C and can I live with the consequences?

Make a list of the pros and cons. Prioritize which considerations are very important to you, and which are less so. Sometimes when you match the pros against the cons you may find them dramatically lopsided.

Solicit opinions and obtain feedback from those you trust or have had a similar situation to contend with. There may be some aspects you haven't thought about.

Make the decision and monitor your results. Make sure you obtain the desired outcome.

Points to Consider

There are no guarantees. Certainly you can never know in advance whether a decision will be correct, therefore, you must be prepared to take risks.

Look for the opportunities. If you make a mistake, view it as an opportunity to learn what didn't work and why. Many times decisions are reversible and you can change your mind.

Hindsight is 20/20. On occasion, you might discover in hindsight situations that may have affected your decision had you known about them earlier. This is normal and typical but should not stall your decision-making process.

Do not get stuck and do nothing. If you've done everything you can to make a good decision and still can't make up your mind, do not delay making an important decision for fear that you don't know enough or will make the wrong choice.

Don't let fear stop you. Sometimes people become so paralyzed with the fear of making a wrong decision that they panic and lose sight of what they're trying to accomplish. This hinders making any decision.

Don't second-guess yourself. In the end second-guessing yourself also undermines what you're trying to accomplish. Once you've made the decision, let the chips fall where they may. At the very least, you will have learned important lessons.

When all is said and done, all you can do is the best with what you have to work with.

Incidentally, do not underestimate the power of intuition, or your gut feeling. After all the facts are weighed and evaluated, it can be the final determinant. Quite often it may be all you have to go by.

DECISION SOLVING STEPS:

Decision making can be easy, just follow these steps:

Ask yourself, what is the real issue?

What are you trying to decide?

Research the facts

Compare the pros and cons

List the positives and negatives for each option

Decide

Choose the option with the greatest number of pros

Take action

Put your decision into action!

Check back

Are you satisfied with the outcome?

Do any adjustments or changes need to be made?

Decision Making Worksheet

Define the question: What are you trying to decide?

_____

_____

Research the facts: Research your options in order to make a decision Based on facts.

_____

_____

_____

Compare the pros and cons for each option!

Complete the Decision Making Chart

Define Question: _____

(What is the question you are trying to answer?)

Pros: (+)	Cons: (-)

Decide

Choose the option with the greatest number of pros.

I choose this option:

_____

_____

_____

_____

Take action

Put your decision into action!

Here is the action I am going to take:

_____

_____

_____

_____

Check back

Are you satisfied with the outcome? Do any adjustments or changes need to be made?

How did my decision work out?

_____

_____

_____

Good luck on your decision!

Chapter Two

Anger Management, Solving Conflicts

Anger Management

"Anger is an acid that can do more harm to the vessel in which it is stored than to anything on which it is poured."

Anger is "an unpleasant emotion ranging from irritation or annoyance to fury or rage."

People experience anger in different ways and for different reasons. Something that makes you furious may only mildly irritate someone else. This subjectivity can make anger difficult to understand and manage. It also highlights that your response to anger is up to you.

It is natural to feel, express, and release anger. However, there are appropriate ways to do so and that's what anger management is all about.

You can get a strong insight into your anger issues by understanding what makes you angry. From there, you can create a plan to minimize frustration and anger in your life.

When you do get angry, there are many approaches you can try to calm down; including changing your environment, using humor, and practicing relaxation techniques. It's also important to release your anger on a regular basis.

Anger is a powerful force that can jeopardize your relationships, your work, and your health, if you don't learn to manage it effectively.

To manage anger, acknowledge that you have a problem, keep an anger log, and build a support network based on trust.

Use techniques to interrupt your anger, listen, empathize, be assertive with others, and learn to relax, as well as laugh at yourself.

Don't let anger get in the way of the joys in life, and learn to forgive people that who make you angry.

Don't let your anger control you. Instead, face it, and take back control of anger and of your life!

Every day, we can experience things that could make us angry. Common causes include feelings of:

Frustration.

Hurt.

Harassment.

Injustice, regardless of whether real or perceived.

Other causes include:

Requests or criticisms that we believe are unfair.

Threats to people, things, or ideas that we hold dear.

Holding onto anger is like drinking poison and expecting the other person to die.

To understand how well you currently manage your anger, take the self-assessment.

How Good Is Your Anger Management? How well do you manage your anger?

Circle "T" for TRUE if you agree with the statement or "F" for FALSE if you disagree with the statement.

T F 1. I use abusive language, such as, name-calling, insults, sarcasm or swearing.

T F 2. People tell me that I become too angry, too quickly.

T F 3. I am easily annoyed and irritated and then it takes a long time to calm down.

T F 4. When I think about the bad things people did to me or the unfair deals that I have gotten in life, I still get angry.

T F 5. I often make critical, judgmental comments to others, even if they do not ask for my advice or help.

T F 6. I use passive-aggressive behaviors, such as ignoring the other person or promising to do something and then "forgetting" about it to get the other person to leave me alone.

T F 7. At times, I use aggressive body language and facial expressions, like clenching my fists, staring at someone, or deliberately looking intimidating.

T F 8. When someone does or says something that angers me, I spend a lot of time thinking about what cutting replies I should have used at the time or how I can get revenge.

T F 9. I use self-destructive behaviors to calm down after an angry outburst such as drinking alcohol or using drugs, gambling, eating too much and vomiting, or cutting myself.

T F 10. When I get really angry about something, I sometimes feel physically sick (headaches, nausea, vomiting, diarrhea, etc.) after the incident.

T F 11. It is very hard to forgive someone who has hurt me even when they have apologized and seem very sorry for having hurt me.

T F 12. I always have to win an argument and prove that I am "right."

T F 13. I usually make excuses for my behavior and blame other people or circumstances for my anger (like job stress, financial problems, etc.)

T F 14. I react to frustration so badly that I cannot stop thinking about it or I can't sleep at night because I think about things that have made me angry.

T F 15. After arguing with someone, I often hate myself for losing my temper.

T F 16. Sometimes I feel so angry that I've thought about killing another person or killing myself.

T F 17. I get so angry that sometimes I forget what I said or did.

T F 18. I know that some people are afraid of me when I get angry or they will "walk on eggshells" to avoid getting me upset.

T F 19. At times I have gotten so angry that I have slammed doors, thrown things, broken items, or punched walls.

T F 20. I have been inappropriately jealous and possessive of my partner, accusing him or her of cheating - even when there was no evidence that my partner was being unfaithful.

T F 21. Sometimes I have forced my partner to do sexual behavior that he or she does not want to do, or I have threatened to cheat on my partner if he/she does not do what I want them to do to please me sexually.

T F 22. At times I have ignored my partner on purpose to hurt him or her, but have been overly nice to other family members or friends.

T F 23. I have kept my partner dependent on me or socially isolated so that I can control and manipulate their feelings and actions so they will not leave me or end our relationship.

T F 24. I have used threats to get my way or win an argument.

T F 25. I feel that people have betrayed me a lot in the past and I have a hard time trusting anyone.

Note: This test is an informal screening test to help you find out more information about your own feelings and expressions of anger. It is not intended to be a formal assessment.

If you answered "true" to 10 or more of these questions, you most likely have moderate-to-severe anger problems.

If you answered "true" to 5 questions, you are most likely at risk for having a problem with your anger.

Even if you answered "true" to just one of the questions, it may be helpful to learn some anger management techniques to improve your coping skills.

If you answered "true" to #16 and feel as if you cannot stop from hurting yourself or someone else, please call 911 for immediate help

Manage Your Anger Constructively

The goal of anger management is not to eliminate anger completely, that isn't possible, since it's a natural human emotion. Rather, the objective is to control and direct your anger so that it doesn't control you, or damage an important relationship or situation.

Understand what causes your anger.

Reduce your angry reactions.

Control your anger when you experience it.

Understand What Causes Your Anger

One of the most effective approaches for managing anger is to identify the sources of the anger you experience. Once you know what makes you angry, you can develop strategies for dealing with it. When you're in the middle of a bad situation, it's hard to think logically and rationally, so understanding what causes your anger can help you plan how to deal with it.

Use a diary or "anger log" to write down the times, people, and situations that make you angry.

Look for trends, or things that make you angry often.

Ask yourself why these things make you angry. Do you connect certain memories to these sources of anger? Do you feel that goals are being frustrated, or that something important to you is being threatened?

Reduce Your Angry Reactions

While you probably won't eliminate anger completely, you can certainly reduce the frequency and scope of your anger. The less angry you are in general, the more control you'll have over your emotions. Since much of our anger can come from frustration and stress, if you work on ways to ease and reduce these causes of frustration and stress, you'll reduce the amount of anger in your life.

Use Problem Solving Skills

A great way to reduce stress is to improve your problem solving skills. We sometimes feel that everything we do needs to be correct and turn out well, and this can be frustrating when things don't turn out as they should. Instead of expecting yourself always to be right, commit to doing your best. That way you can be proud of your effort even if the end result isn't what you want.

Also, accept that when something doesn't work out, the world usually won't end. Sometimes you just need to relax and not let things bother you. We may think that we should have an answer for everything – but the truth is, we don't!

Use Communication Skills

You can also reduce anger by improving your communication skills. When you relate well to other people, express your needs, and talk about issues that bother you, you deal with potential anger proactively.

Build empathy – When you understand another person's perspective, it helps you analyze the situation objectively and understand your role in the conflict. Accept that you may not always know best!

Learn to trust others – Assume the best in people, and don't take their actions personally.

Listen – Use active listening to consider what the other person has to say, and then think before you speak. In many situations, the best way to deal with anger is to accept it, and then find ways to move forward. This can protect your relationships with people, and it allows you to acknowledge your feelings.

Be assertive, not aggressive – By improving your assertiveness skills you can reduce the frustration that you feel when your needs aren't being met. When you know how to ask for what you want, you'll generally feel more in control, and less likely to say things that you'll later regret.

Don't try to communicate when you're still upset

Release Your Anger

You can reduce the likelihood of losing control by releasing the anger that you've built up. When you get rid of angry feelings on a regular basis, you'll feel calmer and more even-tempered, and you'll be more able to deal with the ups and downs of daily life. You can do a variety of things to release your anger, including the following:

Take 10 deep breaths. It really does work!

Do some physical activity – walk, run, swim, play golf, or do some other sport. This can be great for releasing the stress and frustration you've built up!

Use a punching bag or a pillow to physically express your anger (in a way that's not harmful).

Do yoga, or another relaxing form of exercise.

Participate in a fun activity or hobby.

Use a journal and/or art to express your feelings.

Forgive. At some point, it helps to let go and move on with a fresh attitude.

Some people believe that they have to hold their anger in to control it. This is not an effective anger management strategy. Even if you don't show anger to others, that emotion has to go somewhere: it can be stubborn, and it usually doesn't go away on its own.

Control Your Anger When You Experience It

When you start to feel angry, what do you do? Controlling yourself in a bad situation can be difficult, and your actions will have consequences.

External reactions – like kicking and screaming – don't help. You may feel good for a little while, but later, you'll surely feel foolish and sorry. Also, you may do permanent damage to relationships and your reputation.

When you feel that you can't hold your anger in any longer, here are some great strategies to try:

Change Your Environment

Take a break and physically remove yourself from the conflict. Go to another room, go for a walk, or count to 10. This may give you time to gain perspective and simply calm down.

Learn to avoid situations that you know will cause your anger. If you don't like your friend's messy desk, don't go into her office.

If you regularly do something that makes you angry, try to find something else to do in its place. For example, if the crowded elevator upsets you every morning, take the stairs.

Use Humor

Think of something funny to say (but don't be rude or sarcastic).

Try to see the funny side of the situation.

Imagine the other person in a silly situation.

Learn to laugh at yourself.

Smile. It's hard to be angry with a smile on your face.

Calm Yourself Physically.

Use physical relaxation techniques. Take slow, deep breaths and concentrate on your breathing.

Tighten and release small muscle groups. Focus on your hands, legs, back, and toes.

Repeat a word or phrase that reminds you to stay in control and remain confident. For example, say, "I will get through this. Relax! I am doing a great job!"

Practice imagery techniques. Use your imagination or memory to visualize a calming place or situation.

The Dangers of Anger

An appropriate level of anger energizes us to take proper actions, solve problems, and handle situations constructively.

However, uncontrolled anger leads to many negative consequences, especially in the workplace. For instance, it can damage relationships with our bosses and colleagues; and it can lead people to lose trust and respect for us, especially when we react instantly and angrily to something that we've misperceived as a threat.

Anger also clouds our ability to make good decisions and find creative solutions to problems. This can negatively affect our work performance.

Frequent anger poses health risks too. One study found that people who get angry regularly are more likely to suffer from coronary heart disease, eating disorders, and obesity. Research has also found a correlation between anger and premature death. Further studies have found that there is a link between anger and conditions such as anxiety and depression.

Managing Anger

We manage anger when we learn to defuse it before it becomes destructive.

Here are 12 strategies that you can use to control anger when you experience it.

1. Acknowledge that you have a Problem

If you find it difficult to manage your anger, the first thing you need to do is to be honest with yourself and acknowledge that you have a problem. You can then make a plan to deal with it.

2. Keep an Anger Log

Do you know what causes your anger? Chances are, you don't understand why you react angrily to some people or events.

Use the anger log worksheet to monitor the triggers and the frequency of your anger. When you know what makes you angry, you can develop strategies to channel it effectively.

3. Use Your Support Network

Let the important people in your life know about the changes that you're trying to make. They can motivate and support you if you lapse into old behaviors.

These should be give-and-take relationships. Put some time aside every day to invest in these relationships, especially with close friends and family. You need to be there for them, just as they're willing to be there for you.

You can alleviate stress when you spend time with people you care about. This also helps you control your anger.

4. Interrupt the Anger Cycle

When you start to feel angry, try the following techniques:

Yell "Stop!" loudly in your thoughts. This can interrupt the anger cycle.

Use physical relaxation techniques like deep breathing or centering, count to 20 before you respond.

Manage your negative thoughts with imagery and positive thinking.

Close your office door or find a quiet space, and meditate for five minutes.

Distract yourself from your anger, visit your favorite website, play a song that you like, daydream about a hobby that you enjoy, or take a walk.

Another approach is to consider the facts of the situation, so that you can talk yourself out of being angry.

To use this strategy, look at what you can observe about the person or situation, not what you're inferring about someone's motivations or intentions. Does this situation deserve your attention? And is your anger justified here?

When you look only at the facts, you'll likely determine that it's unproductive to respond with anger.

5. Use Empathy

If another person is the source of your anger, use empathy to see the situation from his or her perspective.

Be objective here. Everyone makes mistakes, and it is through mistakes that people learn how to improve.

6. See the Humor in Your Anger

Learn to laugh at yourself and do not take everything seriously. The next time you feel tempted to lash out, try to see the humor in your expressions of anger.

One way to do this is to "catastrophize" the situation. This is when you exaggerate a petty situation that you feel angry about, and then laugh at your self-importance.

For example, imagine that you're angry because a sick team member missed a day of work. As a result, a report you were depending on is now late.

To catastrophize the situation, you think, "Wow, she must have been waiting months for the opportunity to mess up my schedule like this. She and everyone on the team probably planned this, and they're probably sending her updates about how angry I'm getting."

Obviously, this grossly exaggerates the situation. When you imagine a ridiculous and overblown version of the story, you'll likely find yourself smiling by the end of it.

7. Relax

Angry people let little things bother them. If you learn to calm down, you'll realize that there is no real need to get upset, and you'll have fewer angry episodes.

Regular exercise can help you relax in tense situations. When possible, go for a walk, or stretch and breathe deeply whenever you start to feel upset.

You will also feel more relaxed when you get enough sleep and eat a healthy diet.

Dehydration can often lead to irritability too, so keep hydrated throughout the day by drinking plenty of water.

8. Build Trust

Angry people can be cynical. They can believe that others do things on purpose to annoy or frustrate them, even before anything happens. However, people often focus less on you than you might think!

Build trust with friends and colleagues. That way, you'll be less likely to get angry with them when something goes wrong. You'll also be less likely to attribute the problem to malicious intent on their part.

To build trust, be honest with people. Explain your actions or decisions when you need to, and always keep your word. If you do this consistently, people will learn that they can trust you. They'll also follow your lead, and you'll learn that you can trust them in return.

9. Listen Effectively

Miscommunication contributes to frustrating situations. The better you listen to what someone says, the easier it is to find a resolution that doesn't involve an angry response.

So, improve your active listening skills. When others are speaking, focus on what they're saying, and don't get distracted by formulating your response before they've finished. When they're done speaking, show that you listened by reflecting back what they have just said.

10. Be Assertive

Remember, the word is "assertive," not "aggressive." When you're aggressive, you focus on winning. You care little for others' feelings, rights, and needs. When you're assertive, you focus on balance. You're honest about what you want, and you respect the needs of others.

If you're angry, it's often difficult to express yourself clearly. Learn to assert yourself and let other people know your expectations, boundaries, and issues. When you do, you'll find that you develop self-confidence, gain respect, and improve your relationships.

11. Live Each Day as if it's Your Last

Life is short. If you spend all of your time getting angry, you're going to miss the many joys and surprises that life offers.

Think about how many times your anger has destroyed a relationship, or caused you to miss a happy day with friends and family. That's time that you'll never get back.

However, you can prevent this from happening again – the choice is yours.

12. Forgive and Forget

To ensure that you make long-term changes, you need to forgive people who have angered you.

It's not easy to forget past resentments, but the only way to move on is to let go of these feelings. (Depending on what or who is at the root of your anger, you may have to seek a professional's help to achieve this.)

So, start today. Make amends with one person that you've hurt through your anger. It might be difficult, but you'll feel better afterwards. Plus, you'll be one step closer to healing the relationship.

These strategies are only a general guide. If anger continues to be a problem, you might need to seek the help of a suitably qualified health professional, especially if your anger hurts others, or if it causes you physical pain or emotional distress.

CONFLICT Resolution

Conflict happens, it is inevitable. It is going to happen whenever you have people with different expectations. This makes conflict management critical, whether avoiding arguments, disputes, lasting conflict or ultimately, litigation. Conflict can be avoided if steps are taken early in a discussion to diffuse anger and facilitate communication, and it can be resolved by applying a series of thoughtfully applied steps.

Remain Calm

As soon as you realize you're in a conflict with someone, conflict usually consists of strong emotions and even anger but, in such a state, both of you take some time to cool off, then agree on a time and a place to discuss and resolve your conflict.

Stay away from negative talk. Focus on the positive things instead of saying things like, "can't," "don't" or "no." The negative words will only make the conflict harder to resolve.

Be aware of your emotions. If you feel you're getting angry, take a break or figure out a way to calm down. Take a drink of water before you say anything you might regret.

Compromise. In many conflicts, no one person is completely wrong, so try and find a compromise that you can both be happy with.

Make a List of Your Concerns

Before you meet with the other person, sit down and write out exactly what you think led to the conflict because this might lead to a conflict resolution.

Allow the other person to talk. You will still be able to make all of your points, but make sure to let the other person state his or her concerns as well. Let them talk, even if you disagree, because interrupting will only add to the conflict.

Ask Questions

If you don't understand the other person's points, then ask him or her a follow-up question. Make a point to wait until there's a pause in the conversation, so you know the other person has finished stating his or her case and he or she doesn't think you're interrupting. So often, conflict is created and/or maintained because there is no real discussion or debate. We make assumptions about the other person's point of view and willingness to compromise which might be quite wrong

Be Creative

Try to think of as many different solutions to the problem as you can. Both of you should try to think through the conflict before you meet, and then again when you get together and begin your discussion. Allow your discussion to flow in as many different directions as you can, as long as emotions don't get too heated, in order to resolve the conflict effectively.

Take Breaks

If you feel like one of you, or both of you, are getting too emotional, feel free to take as many breaks as you both need to. Take as much time as you need, as soon as voices are raised and before anything too hurtful is said.

Find Something You Can Agree On

There might be a conflict that is just not possible to resolve in one discussion. Think of something to do with the conflict that you both can agree on, and agree to come back to the topic later. It may take more than one discussion to resolve the conflict effectively.

Attack the Problem, Not the Person

However much you disagree with someone, attack the argument, not the person. In truth, most conflict is over matters of little substance and often it is mostly pride or status that is at stake. Your points will be heard more clearly if you can depersonalize your comments and point only at the issue. Rather than accusing people of "always messing things up," it is better to say, "We'll have to take a closer look at why this keeps happening."

Focus on the Future, Not the Past

The present and future tenses are where the solution ends. Rather than focusing on what went wrong or who should have done what, the secret to dispute resolution is to treat it like problem solving and focus on what can be done to resolve the problem.

Be Rational and Pick your Battles

Much conflict is not about substance but perception. Try to clear through the perception to discover and agree on how things really are. Human nature makes us want to be right, even to the point of being defensive or arguing points that do not matter in the big picture. It is even fair game to ask the other person, "On a scale of one-to-ten, how important is this issue to you?"

Seek Mediation If Necessary

This is a process whereby a neutral third party consults with those involved in a conflict to see if the problem can be presented in a way which facilitates a resolution. The mediator may simply listen and ask questions or he/she may suggest other ways of looking at the problem or even possible solutions. Classically this is approach used in most relationship counselling.

If all else fails, wait. Most problems change over time. Either the problem solves itself because circumstances change or one's attitude to the problem changes as the heat dies down and other matters assume more prominence. Therefore, if one cannot solve a dispute and its resolution can wait, maybe the best approach is to leave things alone for a while.

Accept the situation. There is not always a solution waiting to be found and, if there is a solution, it is unlikely to be the only one.

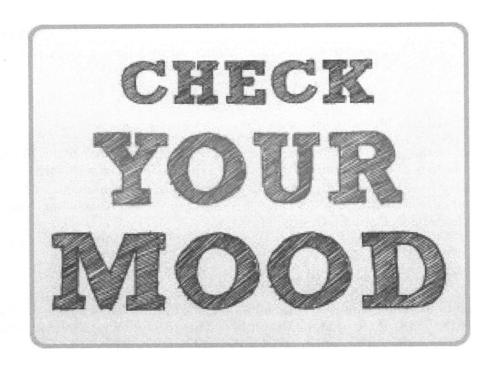

ANGER LOG

Use this form to describe a situation that brought up any type of angry feeling. An angry feeling may be anything from mild annoyance to rage.

Date:_____ **Time:**_____ **Day of Week:** _____

Where were you?

_____

Who were you with?

_____

Briefly describe what happened:

_____

_____

How intense was your anger in this situation?

0	10	20	30	40	50	60	70	80	90	100

None   **Mild**   **Moderate**   **Strong**   **Overpowering**

How long did your anger last? _____ **minutes** _____ **hours** _____ **days**

Thoughts/Appraisals

(Place a check next to each thought that you had)

_____ Demandingness (I thought the other person should have acted differently)

_____ Global Labeling (I thought the other person was "bad," "worthless," "an idiot.")

_____ Catastrophizing (I thought this was one of the worst things that could be occurring)

_____ Over-generalizing (I thought this "always," "every," "never," happening)

_____ Polarized (I thought I was completely right and the other person was completely wrong)

_____ Revenge (I thought this person deserves to suffer or be punished)

_____ Blame (It was the other person's fault that I lost control of my anger)

_____ Misattributions (I thought this person had said or done something to intentionally bother or hurt me)

What physical Sensations did you experience?

_____ Muscle Tension _____ Fluttering in stomach _____ Indigestion _____ Rapid Heart Rate

_____ Nausea _____ Adrenalin Rush _____ Headache _____ Rapid Breathing

_____ Upset Stomach _____ Tingling Sensations _____ Flushing _____ Dizziness

_____ Trembling _____ Sweating _____ Other _____

What Emotions did you experience along with the anger?

_____ Exhausted _____ Depressed _____ Confused _____ Hurt _____ Guilty _____ Lonely

_____ Suspicious _____ Frustrated _____ Shame _____ Sad _____ Disappointed

_____ Embarrassed _____ Desperate _____ Anxious _____ Overwhelmed _____ Numb

_____ Insecure _____ Resentment _____ Other _____

What Behaviors did you engage in when angry?

(Place a check next to each behavior that occurred during this anger episode)

_____ Negative Verbalizations (yelling, swearing, arguing, sarcasm, nasty/abusive remarks)

_____ Bodily Expressions (rolling eyes crossing arms, glaring, frowning, giving stern look)

_____ Passive Retaliation (saying something bad about the person behind his/her back, do

something secretly harmful to the other person, give cold shoulder/ignore)

_____ Hold Anger In (keep things in and boil; harbor resentment and not tell anyone)

_____ Physical Aggression (throw/break object, punch object, hit someone)

_____ Substance Use (drink alcohol, smoke marijuana, misuse of prescription medication)

_____ Try to resolve the situation (compromise, talk through the issue, come to some

agreement with the other person)

In terms of the final and overall outcome of the anger episode, do you believe that:

_____ The overall outcome was generally positive

_____ The overall outcome was neutral

_____ The overall outcome had positive and negative features

_____ The overall outcome was generally negative

Describe why you have rated the outcome in this way. Keep in mind how you could have responded to your feelings of anger differently if the outcome was negative or had negative features.

Chapter Three

Attitude, Behaviors, Problem Solving

Definition of Attitude

A predisposition or a tendency to respond positively or negatively towards a certain idea, object, person, or situation. Attitude influences an individual's choice of action, and responses to challenges, incentives, and rewards (together called stimuli).

An attitude can be as a positive or negative evaluation of people, objects, events, activities, and ideas. Emotion is a common component in persuasion, social influence, and attitude change.

Much of your behavior depends on your attitudes. If your attitudes are negative, you can expect to be vulnerable to addictions and psychosomatic disorders, and the resulting lack of focus and concentration may degrade every area of your life. A positive attitude can be developed by monitoring and disciplining your thoughts on a moment-by-moment basis.

If you have a negative attitude, you can take the steps to change your way of thinking if you really want to. Your attitude has an effect on your life, so changing your negative attitude to a positive one will improve your relationships, job performance and even your health.

Negative thinking appears to be more prevalent than positive thinking. It seems that with most people, positive thinking requires some effort, whereas, negative thinking comes easily and often uninvited. This has much to do with education and the environment one has been living in.

If you have been brought up in a happy and positive atmosphere, there is more probability that it will be easier for you to think positively. However, if you have been brought up under poor or difficult situations, you will more probably be attracted to negative thinking.

You view the world through your predominant mental attitude. If your thoughts are positive, that is fine, but if they are negative, your life and circumstances would probably mirror these thoughts.

If you believe that you are going to fail, you will unconsciously sabotage every opportunity to succeed. If you are afraid of meeting new people or having close relationships, you will do everything to avoid people and relationships, and then complain that you are lonely and nobody loves you.

The power of negative thinking in action

Do you often think about difficulties, failure and disasters?

Do you keep thinking about the negative news that you see and hear on the TV, or read in the newspapers?

Do you see yourself stuck and unable to improve your life or your health?

Do you frequently think that you do not deserve happiness or money, or that it is too difficult to get them?

If you do, then you will close your mind, see no opportunities, and behave and react in such ways, as to repel people and opportunities.

The mind often, doesn't judge or examine thoughts and opinions before accepting them. If what it hears, sees and reads is always negative, it accepts this as a standard.

The media constantly bombards the mind with a lot of information about disasters, catastrophes, wars and other unhappy events. This information sinks into the subconscious mind, and then, manifests as your habitual manner of thinking. By occupying the mind with depressing and pessimistic thoughts you radiate negative energy into the surrounding world, and therefore, create and recreate more negativity, failures and disasters.

The mind is neutral energy. The way you think determines whether the results are positive and beneficial, or negative and harmful. It is the same energy acting in different ways.

The good news is that persistent inner work can change habits of thinking. You must be willing to put energy and time to pursue positive thinking, in order to change your mental attitude.

STOP YOUR STINKIN THINKIN

Tips to Overcome Negative Thinking

Every time you catch yourself thinking a negative thought, replace the thought with a positive one.

If you catch yourself visualizing failure, visualize success instead.

If you hear yourself using negative words in your conversation, switch to positive words.

Instead of saying, "I cannot," say, "I can". Most of the time you can, but choose to say "cannot," due to fear, laziness or lack of self- esteem.

Do you repeat negative words and phrases in your mind? Change them to positive ones. Yes, this requires you to be more alert, and to expend some effort, but you want to change negative thinking into positive thinking don't you?

Allow more positive attitude into your life. Have more faith in yourself and expect positive results. Affirmations and visualization can take you a long way in this direction.

Decide that from today, from this very moment, you are leaving negative thinking behind you, and starting on the way toward positive thinking and behavior

Watch your thoughts, they become words.

Watch your words, they become actions.

Watch your actions, they become habits.

Watch your habits, they become your character.

Watch your character, it becomes your destiny.

Happy positive thinking!

Positive thinking can lead to a lot of positive change in your life. Developing an optimistic outlook can be good for both your physical and mental health. But sometimes, certain situations arise in life that makes it hard to keep a positive outlook. Take steps to make positive thinking become more like second nature and you'll reap some big benefits.

1. Spend Time with Positive People

If you surround yourself with constant complainers, their negativity is likely to rub off on you. Spend time with positive friends and family members to increase the likelihood that their positive thinking habits will become your habits as well. It's hard to be negative when everyone around you is so positive.

2. Take Responsibility for Your Behavior

When you encounter problems and difficulties in life, don't play the role of the victim. Acknowledge your role in the situation and take responsibility for your behavior. Accepting responsibility can help you learn from mistakes and prevent you from blaming others unfairly.

3. Contribute to the Community

One of the best ways to feel good about what you have, is to focus on what you have to give. Volunteer in some manner and give back to the community. Helping others can give you a new outlook on the world and can assist you with positive thinking.

4. Read Positive and Inspirational Material

Spend time each day reading something that encourages positive thinking. Read the Bible, spiritual material, or inspirational quotes to help you focus on what's important to you in life. It can be a great way to start and end your day.

5. Recognize and Replace Negative Thoughts

You won't be successful at positive thinking if you're still plagued by frequent negative thoughts. Learn to recognize and replace thoughts that are overly negative. Often, thoughts that include words like "always" and "never" signal that they aren't true.

If you find yourself thinking something such as, "I always mess everything up," replace it with something more realistic such as, "Sometimes I make mistakes but I learn from them." There's no need to make your thoughts unrealistically positive, but instead, make them more realistic.

6. Establish and Work Toward Goals

It's easier to be positive about problems and setbacks when you have goals that you're working toward. Goals will give you motivation to overcome those obstacles when you encounter problems along the way. Without clear goals, it's harder to make decisions and gauge your progress.

7. Consider the Consequences of Negativity

Spend some time thinking about the consequences of negative thinking. Often, it can become a self-fulfilling prophecy. For example, a person who thinks, "I probably won't get this job interview," may put less effort into the interview. As a result, he may decrease his chances of getting the job.

Create a list of all the ways negative thinking impacts your life. It likely influences your behavior, your relationships, and your feelings. Then, create a list of the ways in which positive thinking could be beneficial.

8. Offer Compliments to Others

Look for reasons to compliment others. Be genuine in your praise and compliments, but offer it frequently. This will help you look for the good in other people.

9. Create a Daily Gratitude List

If you start keeping a daily gratitude list, you'll start noticing exactly how much you have to be thankful for. This can help you focus on the positive in your life instead of thinking about all the bad things that have happened in the day. Getting in the habit of showing an attitude of gratitude makes positive thinking more of a habit.

10. Practice Self-Care

Take good care of yourself and you'll be more equipped to think positively. Get plenty of rest and exercise, manage your stress. Taking care of your physical and mental health will provide you with more energy to focus on positive thinking.

Nowadays, many people's lives are full of worries that have a negative influence both on their lives, and on their positive thinking.

YOU CAN CHANGE YOUR FUTURE BY CHANGING YOUR ATTITUDE

Behavior

The way in which one acts or conducts oneself, especially toward others.

Many things can affect behavior:

Your mood

The people that you are around

Things that happen to you

Stress and your physical condition

Here is a list of words that describe behavior that is good in social situations:

Caring: desire to help people

Charming: pleasant, delightful

Considerate: thinking of others

Enthusiastic: has strong feelings, eager, passion

Excitable: gets excited easily

Faithful: being loyal

Funny: causing people to laugh

Kind: thoughtful, caring

Pleasant: polite, nice

Polite: exhibiting good manners

Sincere: being totally honest

Thoughtful: thinking things over

For the opposite kind of behavior, here is a list of words that refer to bad social behavior:

Aggressive: verbally or physically threatening

Argumentative: often arguing with people

Bossy: always telling people what to do

Deceitful: doing or saying anything to get people to do what you want or to get what you want

Domineering: constantly trying to control others

Inconsiderate: not caring about others or their feelings

Irritating: bothering people

Manic: acting just a little crazy

Manipulative: always trying to influences other people

Moody: being unpredictable, changing moods often

Rude: treating people badly, breaking social rules

Spiteful: seeking revenge, hurting others because you didn't get what you want

Thoughtless: not thinking about the effects of your actions or words

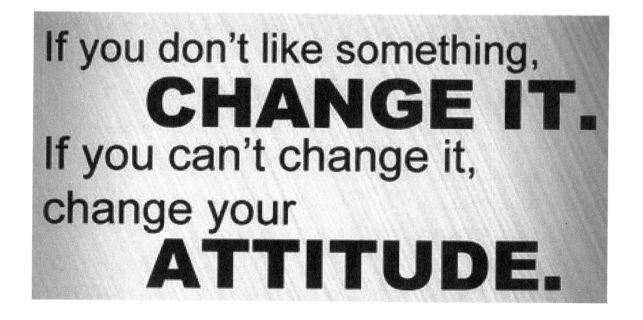

THE PROBLEM-SOLVING PROCESS

Problem-solving is a tool, a skill, and a process. As a tool it helps you solve a problem or achieve a goal. As a skill you can use it repeatedly throughout your life. And, as a process it involves a number of steps. It is not unusual for problems to arise when you are working towards a goal and encounter obstacles along the way.

Step 1 - Problem Definition

Before you are ready to take any steps to solve the problem, you first have to be sure that you are clear about what the problem really is. It can be easy to get distracted by solving a different problem than what is actually causing distress if it is easier than dealing with the real problem.

This step involves thinking about the following questions:

How is the current situation different from what I actually want it to be?

What do I actually want, or how do I actually want things to be?

What is preventing me from achieving my goals, or from things being the way I want them to be?

Step 2 - Problem Analysis

Once you have defined the problem, you need to think about it from different perspectives to insure that you understand all the dimensions of the problem.

The following questions can be useful to help you analyze the problem.

How is this problem affecting me?

How is this problem affecting other people?

Who else is experiencing this problem?

How do other people deal with this problem?

Step 3 - Establish Your Goals

Once you have looked at the problem from different perspectives, you can decide what you want to achieve and establish your goals. You need to answer the very specific question – "What is my immediate goal?"

Step 4 - Generate Possible Solutions

During this stage the goal is to generate as many possible solutions as you can. Do not worry about whether or not they are realistic, practical, or effective. Frequently a solution you might eliminate initially, with work can be developed into a very effective solution.

Step 5 - Analyze the Solution

During this stage, you will examine each alternative and write down both the advantages and disadvantages to each. Some considerations to keep in mind include:

Is it relevant to my situation?

Is it realistic?

Is it manageable?

What are the consequences – both good and bad?

What is the likelihood that it is going to help me reach my goal?

Step 6 - Implementation

The last step is to implement the solution you have chosen. This step involves identification of all the steps necessary to implement it, and also on-going monitoring of the effectiveness of the solution to make sure that it actually solved the problem. During this stage of the process, ask yourself the following questions:

How effective is the solution?

Did it achieve what I wanted?

What consequences (good and bad) did it have in my situation?

If the solution was successful in helping you solve your problem, then you can feel satisfied with your efforts and what you learned. If you feel dissatisfied in some way, you can either modify the solution to work better, or you can scrap it and turn to other alternative solutions, or begin the process again.

Remember that problem-solving is a cycle – it involves searching for a solution to a problem that will lead to various possible solutions which then need to be evaluated

Steps to solve a problem...

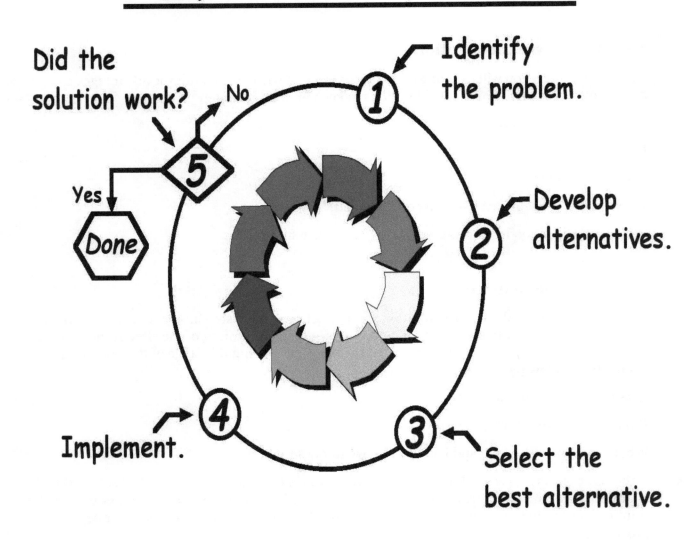

Did the
solution work?

No

Identify
the problem.

Yes

Done

Develop
alternatives.

Implement.

Select the
best alternative.

1

2

3

4

5

SELF IMPROVEMENT

"Nobody can go back and start a new beginning, but anyone can start today and make a new ending."

Nothing is more important than how you feel and think about yourself.

A high opinion about yourself and who you are and what you do and basically a love for yourself is also one of the things that people often miss or have too little of in today's society.

1. Say stop to your inner critic

A good place to start with raising your self-esteem is by learning how to handle and to replace the voice of your own inner critic.

We all have an inner critic.

It can spur you on to get things done or to do things to gain acceptance from the people in your life. But at the same time it will drag your self-esteem down.

This inner voice whispers or shouts destructive thoughts in your mind.
Thoughts for example:

You are lazy and sloppy, now get to work.

You aren't good at your job at all and someone will figure that out and throw you out.

You are worse or uglier than your friend/co-worker/partner.

You don't have to accept this though. There are ways to minimize that critical voice and to replace it with more helpful thoughts. You can change how you view yourself.

One way to do so is simply to say stop whenever the critic pipes up in your mind.

You can do this by creating a stop-word or stop-phrase.

As the critic says something – in your mind – shout: STOP!

Or use this favorite: No, no, no, we are not going there!

Or come up with a phrase or word that you like that stops the train of the thought driven by the inner critic.

Then refocus your thoughts to something more constructive. Like planning what you want to eat for dinner or your tactic for the next soccer game.

In the long run it also helps a lot to find better ways to motivate yourself than listening to your inner critic. So let's move on to that...

49

2. Use healthier motivation habits

To make the inner critic less useful for yourself and that voice weaker and at the same time motivate yourself to take action and raise your self-esteem it is certainly helps to have healthy motivation habits.

Remind yourself of the benefits. A simple but powerful way to motivate yourself and to keep that motivation up daily is to write down the deeply felt benefits you will get from following this new path or reaching a goal.

Like for example getting into better shape and having more energy for your kids and the people close to you. Or making more money and through that being able to travel with the love of your life and experience wonderful new things together.

When your list is done then save it and put it somewhere where you will see it every day. For instance in your workspace or on your fridge.

Refocus on doing what YOU really, really like to do. When you really, really like doing something then the motivation to do that thing tends to comes pretty automatically. When you really want something in life then it also becomes easier to push through any inner resistance you feel.

So if you lose your motivation, ask yourself: Am I doing what I really want to do? If not and if possible, then refocus and start working on that very important thing instead.

After you have used your stop-word or phrase focus on one of these techniques. Over time it will become a habit and your inner critic will pop up a lot less often.

3. Take a 2 minute self-appreciation break

This is a very simple and fun habit. And if you spend just two minutes on it every day for a month then it can make huge difference.

Here's what you do:

Take a deep breath, slow down and ask yourself this question: what are 3 things I can appreciate about myself?

A few examples are:

I like to help other people.

I can make people laugh and forget about their troubles.

I am very thoughtful and caring when it comes to our pets.

These things don't have to be big things.

Maybe just that you listened fully for a few minutes to someone who needed it today. That you took a healthy walk or bike ride after work. That you are a caring and kind person in many situations.

These short breaks do not only build self-esteem in the long run but can also turn a negative mood around and reload you with a lot of positive energy again.

4. Write down 3 things in the evening that you can appreciate about yourself

This is a variation of the habit above and combining the two of them can be extra powerful for two boosts in self-esteem a day.

Or you may simply prefer to use this variation at the end of your day when you have some free time for yourself to spare.

What you do is to ask yourself the question from the last section:

What are 3 things I can appreciate about myself?

Write down your answers every evening in a journal made out of paper or on your computer/smart phone.

A nice extra benefit of writing it down is that after a few weeks you can read through all the answers to get a good self-esteem boost and change in perspective on days when you may need it the most.

5. Do the right thing

When you do what you deep down think is the right thing to do then you raise and strengthen your self-esteem.

It might be a small thing like getting up from the couch and going to the gym. It could be to be understanding instead of judgmental in a situation. Or to stop feeling sorry for yourself and focus on the opportunities and gratitude for what you actually have.

It is not always easy to do. Or even to know what the right thing is. But keeping a focus on it and doing it as best you can makes big difference both in the results you get and for how you think about yourself.

One tip that makes it easier to stay consistent with doing the right thing is to try to take a few such actions early in the day. Like for example giving someone a compliment, eating a healthy breakfast and working out.

This sets the tone for the rest of your day.

6. Replace the perfectionism

Thought habits can be as destructive in daily life as perfectionism.

It can paralyze you from taking action because you become so afraid of not living up to some standards. You then procrastinate and you do not get the results you want. This will make your self-esteem sink.

Or you take action but are never or very rarely satisfied with what you accomplished and your own performance. Your opinion and feelings about yourself become more and more negative and your motivation to take action plummets.

How can you overcome perfectionism?

Go for good enough. When you aim for perfection then that usually winds up in a project or a task never being finished. So simply go for good enough instead. Don't use it as an excuse to slack off. But simply realize that there is something called good enough and when you are there then you are finished.

Remember that buying into myths of perfection will hurt you and the people in your life. This simple reminder that life is not like in a movie, a song or a book can be good reality check whenever you are daydreaming of perfection. Because reality can clash with your expectations when they are out of this world and harm or even possibly lead to the end of relationships, jobs, projects and so on.

7. Handle mistakes and failures in a more positive way

If you go outside of your comfort zone, if you try to accomplish anything that is truly meaningful then you will stumble and fall along the way.

That is OK. It is normal. Most people have failed many times before they have succeeded. We just don't always hear about it as much as we hear about their successes.

So remember that. And when you stumble try this:

Be your own best friend. Instead of beating yourself up, ask yourself: How would my friend/parent support me and help me in this situation? Then do things and talk to yourself like he/she would. It keeps you from falling into a pit of despair and helps you to be more constructive after the first initial pain of a mistake or failure starts to dissipate.

Find the upside. Another way to be more constructive in this kind of situation is to focus on optimism and opportunities. So ask yourself: what is one thing I can learn from this? And what is one opportunity I can find in this situation? This will help you to change your viewpoint and hopefully not hit the same bump a little further down the road.

8. Be kind towards other people

When you are kinder towards others you tend to treat and think of yourself in a kinder way too. And the way you treat other people is how they tend to treat you in the long run.

So focus on being kind in your daily life.

You can for example:

Just be there and listen as you let someone vent.

Hold the door open for the next person.

Let someone into your lane while driving.

Encourage a friend or a family member when they are uncertain or unmotivated.

Take a few minutes help someone out in a practical way.

9. Try something new

When you try something new, when you challenge yourself in a small or bigger way and go outside of your comfort zone then your opinion of yourself goes up.

You may not have done whatever you did in a spectacular or great way but you at least tried instead of sitting on your hands and doing nothing.

And that is something to appreciate about yourself and it can help you come alive as you get out of a rut.

Go outside of your comfort zone regularly. Don't expect anything, just tell yourself that you will try something different.

Later on you can do the same thing a few more times and improve your own performance.

And as always, if it feels too scary or uncomfortable then don't beat yourself up. Take a smaller step forward instead by gently nudging yourself into motion.

10. Stop falling into the comparison trap

When you compare your life, yourself and what you have to other people's lives and what they have then you have destructive habit on your hands.

Because you can never win. There is always someone who has more or is better than you at something in the world. There are always people ahead of you.

Look at how far you have come. Compare yourself to yourself. Focus on you. On your results and on how you can and how you have improved your results. This will both motivate you and raise your self-esteem.

11. Spend more time with supportive people and less time with destructive people

Even if you focus on being kinder towards other people (and yourself) and on replacing a perfectionism habit it will be hard to keep your self-esteem up if the most important influences in your life drag it down on a daily or weekly basis.

So make changes in the input you get. Choose to spend less time with people who are nervous perfectionists, unkind or unsupportive of your dreams or goals. And spend more time with positive, uplifting people who have more human and kinder standards and ways of thinking about things.

And think about what you read, listen to and watch too. Spend less time on an internet blog, reading a magazine or watching a TV-show if you feel it makes you unsure of yourself and if it makes you feel more negatively towards yourself.

Spend the time you used to spend on this information source on for example reading positive books, blogs, websites and listening to podcasts that help you and that make you feel good about yourself.

12. Remember the whys of high self-esteem

What is a simple way to stay consistent with doing something?

Remember the most important reasons you are doing it.

Remind yourself of the whys and help yourself stay motivated. Work on your self-esteem and make it an essential priority.

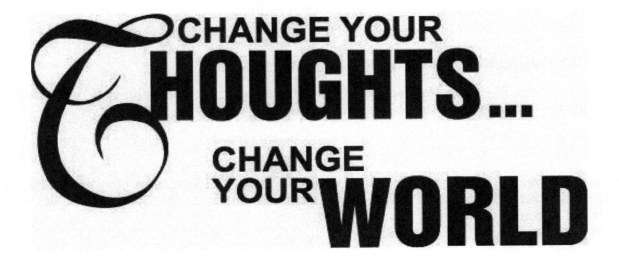

Chapter Four

Setting Goals,
Identifying Strengths and Skills

Setting Goals and Staying on Course

Once you've decided on your first set of goals, keep the process going by reviewing and updating your To-Do List on a daily basis. Periodically review the longer term plans, and modify them to reflect your changing priorities and experience.

SMART Goals

A useful way of making goals more powerful is to use the SMART mnemonic. While there are plenty of variants (some of which are included in parenthesis), SMART usually stands for:

S - Specific (or Significant).

M - Measurable (or Meaningful).

A - Attainable (or Action-Oriented).

R - Relevant (or Rewarding).

T - Time-bound (or Track-able).

Further Goal Setting Tips

State each goal as a positive statement - Express your goals positively.

Be precise: Set precise goals, putting in dates, times and amounts so that you can measure achievement. If you do this, you'll know exactly when you have achieved the goal, and can take complete satisfaction from having achieved it.

Set priorities: When you have several goals, give each a priority. This helps you to avoid feeling overwhelmed by having too many goals, and helps to direct your attention to the most important ones.

Write goals down: This crystallizes them and gives them more force.

Keep operational goals small - Keep the low-level goals that you're working towards small and achievable. If a goal is too large, then it can seem that you are not making progress towards it. Keeping goals small and incremental gives more opportunities for reward.

Set performance goals, not outcome goals - You should take care to set goals over which you have as much control as possible. It can be quite dispiriting to fail to achieve a personal goal for reasons beyond your control!

Set realistic goals – It's important to set goals that you can achieve. All sorts of people (for example, employers, parents, media, or society) can set unrealistic goals for you. They will often do this in ignorance of your own desires and ambitions.

It's also possible to set goals that are too difficult because you might not appreciate either the obstacles in the way, or understand quite how much skill you need to develop to achieve a particular level of performance.

Why Set Goals?

Goal setting is used by top-level athletes, successful business-people and achievers in all fields. Setting goals gives you long-term vision and short-term motivation. It focuses your acquisition of knowledge, and helps you to organize your time and your resources so that you can make the very most of your life.

By setting sharp, clearly defined goals, you can measure and take pride in the achievement of those goals, and you'll see forward progress in what might previously have seemed a long pointless grind. You will also raise your self-confidence, as you recognize your own ability and competence in achieving the goals that you've set.

Starting to Set Personal Goals

You set your goals on a number of levels:

First you create your "big picture" of what you want to do with your life (or over the next 10 years), and identify the large-scale goals that you want to achieve.

Then, you break these down into the smaller and smaller targets that you must hit to reach your lifetime goals.

Finally, once you have your plan, you start working on it to achieve these goals.

This is why we start the process of goal setting by looking at your lifetime goals. Then, we work down to the things that you can do in, say, the next five years, then next year, next month, next week, and today, to start moving towards them.

Step 1: Setting Lifetime Goals

The first step in setting personal goals is to consider what you want to achieve in your lifetime (or at least, by a significant and distant age in the future). Setting lifetime goals gives you the overall perspective that shapes all other aspects of your decision making.

To give a broad, balanced coverage of all important areas in your life, try to set goals in some of the following categories (or in other categories of your own, where these are important to you):

Career - What level do you want to reach in your career, or what do you want to achieve?

Financial - How much do you want to earn, by what stage? How is this related to your career goals?

Education - Is there any knowledge you want to acquire in particular? What information and skills will you need to have in order to achieve other goals?

Family - Do you want to be a parent? If so, how are you going to be a good parent? How do you want to be seen by a partner or by members of your extended family?

Artistic - Do you want to achieve any artistic goals?

Attitude - Is any part of your mindset holding you back? Is there any part of the way that you behave that upsets you? (If so, set a goal to improve your behavior or find a solution to the problem.)

Physical - Are there any athletic goals that you want to achieve, or do you want good health deep into old age? What steps are you going to take to achieve this?

Pleasure - How do you want to enjoy yourself? (You should ensure that some of your life is for you!)

Public Service - Do you want to make the world a better place? If so, how?

Spend some time brainstorming these things, and then select one or more goals in each category that best reflect what you want to do. Then consider trimming again so that you have a small number of really significant goals that you can focus on.

As you do this, make sure that the goals that you have set are ones that you genuinely want to achieve, not ones that your parents, family, or employers might want. (If you have a partner, you probably want to consider what he or she wants - however, make sure that you also remain true to yourself!)

SMART GOALS

Specific

Goals should be straightforward and emphasize what you want to happen. Specifics help us to focus our efforts and clearly define what we are going to do. Specific is the What, Why, and How of the SMART model.

WHAT are you going to do? Use action words such as direct, organize, coordinate, lead, develop, plan, build etc.

WHY is this important to do at this time? What do you want to ultimately accomplish?

HOW are you going to do it? (By...)

Ensure the goals you set is very specific, clear and easy. Instead of setting a goal to lose weight or be healthier, set a specific goal to lose 2inches off my waistline or to walk 5 miles at an aerobically challenging pace.

Measurable

If you can't measure it, you can't manage it. In the broadest sense, the whole goal statement is a measure for the project; if the goal is accomplished, this is a success. However, there are usually several short-term or small measurements that can be built into the goal. Choose a goal with measurable progress, so you can see the change occur. How will you see when you reach your goal? Be specific! "I want to read 3 chapter books of 100 pages on my own before my birthday" shows the specific target to be measure. "I want to be a good reader" is not as measurable.

Establish concrete criteria for measuring progress toward the attainment of each goal you set. When you measure your progress, you stay on track, reach your target dates, and experience the exhilaration of achievement that spurs you on to continued effort required to reach your goals.

Attainable

When you identify goals that are most important to you, you begin to figure out ways you can make them come true. You develop the attitudes, abilities, skills, and financial capacity to reach them. Your begin seeing previously overlooked opportunities to bring yourself closer to the achievement of your goals. Goals you set which are too far out of your reach, you probably won't commit to doing. Although you may start with the best of intentions, the knowledge that it's too much for you means your subconscious will keep reminding you of this fact and will stop you from even giving it your best. A goal needs to stretch you slightly so you feel you can do it and it will need a real commitment from you. For instance, if you aim to lose 20lbs in one week, we all know that isn't achievable. But setting a goal to loose 1lb and when you've achieved that, aiming to lose a further 1lb, will keep it achievable for you. The feeling of success which this brings helps you to remain motivated.

Realistic

This is not a synonym for "easy." Realistic, in this case, means "do-able." It means that the learning curve is not a vertical slope; that the skills needed to do the work are available; that the project fits with the overall strategy and goals of the organization. A realistic project may push the skills and knowledge of the people working on it but it shouldn't break them. Devise a plan or a way of getting there which makes the goal realistic. The goal needs to be realistic for you and where you are at the moment. A goal of never again eating sweets, cakes, crisps and chocolate may not be realistic for someone who really enjoys these foods. For instance, it may be more realistic to set a goal of eating a piece of fruit each day instead of one sweet item. You can then choose to work towards reducing the amount of sweet products gradually as and when this feels realistic for you. Be sure to set goals that you can attain with some effort! Too difficult and you set the stage for failure, but too low sends the message that you aren't very capable. Set the bar high enough for a satisfying achievement!

Timely

Set a time-frame for the goal: next week, in three months, in one year. Putting an end point on your goal gives you a clear target to work towards. If you don't set a time, the commitment is too vague. It tends not to happen because you feel you can start at any time. Without a time limit, there's no urgency to start taking action now. Time must be measurable, attainable and realistic. Everyone will benefit from goals and objectives if they are SMART. SMART, is the instrument to apply in setting your goals and objectives.

SMART Goals

Specific	What **exactly** will you do?
Measurable	How will you know if you **meet** your goal?
Achievable	What **steps** are you going to take to reach your goal?
Relevant	What about your goal makes it **important** to you?
Timely	**When** do you want to complete your goal?

What are your strengths?

You don't have to be a super hero to have super powers. Everyone has strengths.

In fact, knowing your natural talents, skills, abilities and personal accomplishments will bring you one step closer to knowing what you want to do to achieve your goals.

Some strengths make tasks feel almost effortless such as good eye-hand coordination, reasoning skills or understanding information. Other strengths can be developed and improved over time, like learning to budget your money or to solve everyday problems. Skills often require some form of instruction and practice such as desktop publishing or applying geometry. The point is that you can continue to acquire and build your skills throughout your life.

"STRENGTH, A river cuts through a rock, not because of its power but its persistence"

How to Identify Your Strengths and Weaknesses

Knowing where you come in strong and where you need assistance can help you stabilize your personal life and nurture your professional interactions. Self-knowledge is a powerful tool that too many people disregard because it's difficult or inconvenient. If you want to be able to identify your strengths and weaknesses, whether for a job or for person reasons.

1. Identify Your Strengths and Weaknesses

Throw away the "weaknesses" that are really just strengths in disguise. Potential employers are not stupid, and can see right through this. They interview sometimes hundreds of people for a position, and everyone's first instinct is to use a strength and spin it as a weakness.

"Strengths" that are commonly spun as "weaknesses" include:

"I'm a perfectionist and I can't stand to get things wrong."

"I'm stubborn and I don't let things go."

"I struggle to maintain a good work/life balance because I work so hard."

Instead, identify a real weakness. Weaknesses are human. There wouldn't be any point in asking the question if all you gave the interviewer was some silly response about how awesome you are. Real weaknesses might include:

Being overly critical

Being suspicious (of authority, of peers)

Being too demanding

Procrastinating

Being too talkative

Being too sensitive

Exhibiting a lack of assertiveness

Exhibiting a lack of social tact

Acknowledge the bad parts of your weakness, and how they could affect your performance. It can be quite impressive to talk about how your weakness has affected or could potentially affect your work performance. It shows insight and truthfulness, although you still need to be tactful about what you say.

Talk about your strengths confidently, without being cocky. Try to be confident while still staying humble about your achievements and skills. Of course, try to truthfully pick strengths that could be in line with the individual, business, or organization to which you are applying. *Real strengths fall into three main categories:*

Knowledge Based Skills: computer skills, languages, technical know-how, etc.

Transferable Skills: communication and people management skills, problem solving, etc.

Personal Traits: sociability, confidence, punctuality, etc.

2. Personal Development

Each of us possess certain strengths and weaknesses. They shape and may even dictate how we approach life. Strengths are considered to be the talents, innate abilities and desires that "click" for you. In other words, these are the things that you'd be tempted to say "It wasn't effort, I've always had the ability to...."

Strengths should not be confused with skills, which can be learned or improved. For example, confidence and assertiveness are skills, while a way with words is probably a strength.

Weaknesses are considered to be something about yourself that you have the power to improve. It might be professional or social skills, or poor self-restraint when it comes to food. Often this aspect is about "learning lessons from life" and not repeating mistakes; other times, it's about making the effort to overcome a lack of skills.

Consider how you respond in certain situations that require action, thought and insight. Before doing anything more concrete, try to monitor your spontaneous reactions to experiences you've had in life already. The reason for doing this is that the spontaneous reactions tell you a lot about how you react in both ordinary and intense situations. Ask yourself the following series of questions on how you would respond and use your gut feeling.

Think of a challenging situation in which something bad happened. Perhaps it's a plane plummeting in turbulence or a child suddenly dashing out in front of your car while you slam on your brakes. How did you react when confronted with the spontaneous situation? Do you clam up and retreat or do you meet the challenge head on, assembling tools and resources to address the situation?

If you took control and acted as a leader, you probably feel that handling these situations is a strength. If you reacted by crying uncontrollably, feeling helpless or lashing out at others, staying in self-control during a challenging situation might be a weakness.

Think of less challenging situations that are still hard but not so life and death. For example, how do you react when you enter a crowded room? Do you want to engage everyone you meet there or do you want to find a quiet corner away from the noise and connect with just one person?

The person connecting with others is strong at socializing, while the quieter person is strong at connecting individually. Both of these strengths can be used to the person's natural advantage.

It might not be effective to call either relational style a weakness, although in certain situations, shyness can be a weakness. The silver lining is that the "weaknesses" can be improved upon.

3. Thought Exercises

Think of a time when you've been put on the spot and had to react immediately. How quickly do you learn and adapt to new situations? Are you a fast thinker, rattling off a great comeback when a co-worker makes a snide remark? Or do you tend to absorb, think, and then react in those situations?

The person who rattles off a brilliant comeback or who solves a problem quickly can be said to have quick-wittedness as a strength, and perhaps limited depth as a weakness.

The person who takes time to think could be described as having planning as a strength and perhaps limited nimbleness as a weakness.

Think of a time when you had to make a decision but lacked all of the facts. Maybe you're asked to design a marketing strategy for a part of the world you know nothing about. How do you react?

If you go ahead and make the decision without waiting to gather all the information, your strength might be in taking practical action as a means to clarify a situation. Your weakness might be shortsightedness.

On the other hand, if you waited until you got more facts before making the decision, your strength may be in analysis and certainty, while your weakness may be over-cautiousness.

4. Consider Your Desires

Your desires or longings say a lot about you, even if you've been spending a lot of time denying them. Stories abound of people pursuing a particular career course because it's what their family expected, and becoming a doctor or lawyer when they'd rather have been a ballet dancer or a mountain trekker instead.

Ask yourself: What are your desires in life? Whether you're applying for your first job or have just settled into retirement, you should always have goals and yearnings in life. Determine what drives you and what makes you happy.

Consider why you want to complete those activities or goals and what it will take to reach them. Chances are, these are your passions and dreams in life, your areas of great strength.

Ask yourself: What types of activities do you find satisfying or appealing? For some, sitting by the fire with a good book is extremely satisfying. For others, sitting fireside with a book sounds very dull, they'd rather be rock climbing or taking a road trip.

Make a list of the activities or things you do that make you happy and provide you with pleasure, most likely, those are some strong areas for you.

Ask yourself: When do you feel energized and motivated? Consider times in your life when you feel ready to take the world on by storm or inspired to go to the next level. The areas that inspire and motivate you are typically where you are strongest.

Note that many people feel desires very early on in life, indicating the childlike self-knowledge that many come to lose when family, peer and social expectations or financial pressures push the initial desires down deep.

Write down areas of your work and life that you believe or think are your strong and weak areas. This time you're being asked to consciously focus on making choices about how you currently see your own strengths and weaknesses. This should be based on what you're doing in your life right now, both personal and professional, rather than looking to the past or to your desires. And remember, no one is grading this "test" or judging you based on your responses, so be honest! Write down your strengths and weaknesses on the worksheet on page 71.

See worksheet

5. Compare and Reflect

Compare the lists against one another. Did they match up and did you find any surprises?

Consider any surprises or mismatches across the lists you've made in the preceding steps. Reflect on why you think that some of the qualities and weaknesses you've spotted have turned out to be different. Some are based on your "gut," some on your "desires," and some are based on what you "think." Is it possible that you think you enjoy certain things or that you're motivated by certain things, but in actuality you can't or you aren't?

Focus on those areas that differ and try to identify situations that address the area.

Have a close friend or family member provide you with feedback. Although self-examination can lead you to a few answers, getting an outside opinion will help you either solidify your observations or can shatter a few illusions too.

Choose someone who will give you the truth and not sugarcoat or gloss over your weaknesses. Find an external, neutral person, preferably a peer or a mentor, to give you honest feedback.

Ask for feedback on your lists. Have your outside person review and comment on your lists. Helpful comments and questions may include, "What makes you think that you don't act quickly in emergency situations?" The outside observer may recall an instance where you were the hero of the day during an emergency although you may have forgotten.

Reflect and determine how you feel about your identified strengths and weaknesses. Decide if you need or want to work on any of your weaknesses and contemplate what you will need to do to attack or change any weaknesses.

Enroll in a class or find activities that will address your weaknesses. For example, if you find that you become a deer in headlights when confronted with a spontaneous situation, put yourself in situations where spontaneity occurs. Examples including joining an adult community theater, participating on a sports team, or even doing karaoke at the bar.

Consider therapy or ways to talk about fears or concerns. If taking a class or joining a theater group doesn't seem to do the trick, and you have deep rooted fears or anxiety that prevent you from moving forward, consider talking with a therapist.

Take care not to become hung up on weaknesses. Some of them are best accepted rather than worked on. You can spend too much time trying to over-correct a weakness at the expense of celebrating a strength that compensates for the weakness.

Don't deny the "WOW" moments in your life. These are the times when you do something you've never done before and it just "clicks," and you find that you're a total natural at it. This might be sports, art, creative pursuits, interacting with animals, standing in for someone who is away and doing their job, etc. If you suddenly discover a fire inside yourself and an ability to do something as if you were born to do it, it's highly likely that you've fallen onto a previously undiscovered strength. Not everyone will experience this amazing moment, but if you do, work with it to enhance your life and reach your true potential.

What are Skills?

Skills are simply the things you learn, that enable you to perform certain tasks.

By knowing the "language" of skills, you can communicate them to others by understanding, describing, and discussing them. This happens when you:

Write a resume,

Read about a job opening,

Go for a job interview,

Talk with your supervisor,

Ask for a raise,

Seek a promotion,

Change your career, or

Learn new skills.

To succeed in this high-performance, global economy, everyone needs to understand and be good at communicating about skills; students, employers, employees, job seekers, educators, and human resource managers. Your success requires continuous improvement, strengthening and learning new skills. Start directing your own skills education and you're making the first step by reading this program!

There are four groups of Foundation Skills:

Basic Skills, Thinking Skills, People Skills, Personal Qualities

1. Basic Skills

Reading: Identify relevant details, facts, and specification; locate information in books/manuals, from graphs; find meaning of unknown words; judge accuracy of reports; use computer to find information.

Writing: Write ideas completely and accurately in letters and reports with proper grammar, spelling, and punctuation; check, edit, and revise for accuracy and emphasis, use computer to communicate information.

Mathematics: Use numbers, fractions, and percentages to solve problems; use tables, graphs, diagrams, and charts; use computer to enter, retrieve, change, and communicate numerical information.

Speaking: Organize and communicate ideas clearly; speak clearly; select language, tone of voice, and gestures appropriate to audience.

Listening: Listen carefully to what person says, noting tone of voice, and other body language; respond in a way that shows understanding of what is said.

2. Thinking Skills

Creative Thinking: Use imagination freely, combining ideas or information in new ways; make connections between ideas that seem unrelated.

Problem-Solving Skills: Recognize problem; identify why it is a problem; create and implement a solution; watch to see how well solution works; revise as needed.

Decision Making Skills: Identify goal; generate alternatives and gather information about them; weigh pros and cons; choose best alternative; plan how to carry out the choice.

Visualization: See a building or object by looking at a blueprint, drawing, or sketch; imagine how a system works by looking at a schematic drawing.

3. People Skills

Social: Show understanding, friendliness, and respect for feelings; assert oneself when appropriate; take an interest in what people say and why they think and act as they do.

Negotiation: Identify common goals among different parties in conflict; clearly present the facts and arguments of your position; listen to and understand other party's position; create possible ways to resolve conflict; make reasonable compromises.

Leadership: Communicate thoughts and feelings to justify a position; encourage or convince others; make positive use of rules or values; demonstrate ability to have others believe in and trust you because of your competence and honesty.

Teamwork: Work cooperatively with others; contribute to the group with ideas and effort; do your own share of the work; encourage team members; resolve differences for the benefit of the team; responsibly challenge existing procedures, policies, or authorities.

Cultural Diversity: Work well with people having different ethnic, social, or educational backgrounds; understand the concerns of members of other ethnic and gender groups; base impressions on a person's behavior, not stereotypes; understand one's own culture and those of others and how they differ; respectfully help people in these groups make cultural adjustments when necessary.

4. Personal Qualities

Self-Esteem: Understand how beliefs affect how a person feels and acts; "listen" to and identify irrational or harmful beliefs you may have; and understand how to change these negative beliefs when they occur.

Self-Management: Assess your knowledge and skills accurately; set specific, realistic personal goals; monitor progress toward your goal.

Responsibility: Work hard to reach goals, even if the task is unpleasant; do quality work; display high standard of attendance, honesty, energy, and optimism.

What are Interpersonal Skills?

We've all been developing our interpersonal skills since childhood - usually subconsciously.

Interpersonal skills are the life skills we use every day to communicate and interact with other people, both individually and in groups. People who have worked on developing strong interpersonal skills are usually more successful in both their professional and personal lives.

Employers often seek to hire staff with "strong interpersonal skills". They want people who will work well in a team and be able to communicate effectively with colleagues, customers and clients.

A List of Interpersonal Skills Includes:

Verbal Communication - What we say and how we say it.

Non-Verbal Communication - What we communicate without words, body language is an example.

Listening Skills - How we interpret both the verbal and non-verbal messages sent by others.

Negotiation - Working with others to find a mutually agreeable outcome.

Problem Solving - Working with others to identify, define and solve problems.

Decision making- Exploring and analyzing options to make sound decisions.

Assertiveness- Communicating our values, ideas, beliefs, opinions, needs and wants freely.

Interpersonal Skills become so natural that we may take them for granted, never thinking about how we communicate with other people. With a little time and effort you can develop these skills. Good interpersonal skills can improve many aspects of your life - professionally and socially - they lead to better understanding and relationships.

Interpersonal skills are also sometimes referred to as: social skills, people skills, soft skills, communication skills or life skills. Although these terms can include interpersonal skills they tend to be broader and therefore may also refer to other types of skills.

Learn to Listen

Listening is not the same as hearing. Take time to listen carefully to what others are saying through both their verbal and non-verbal communication

Choose Your Words

Be aware of the words you are using when talking to others. Could you be misunderstood or confuse the issue? Practice clarity and learn to seek feedback to ensure your message has been understood.

Understand Why Communication Fails

Communication is rarely perfect and can fail for a number of reasons. Learn about the various barriers to good communication so you can be aware of and reduce the likelihood of ineffective interpersonal communication and misunderstandings.

Relax

When we are nervous we tend to talk more quickly and therefore less clearly. Being tense is also evident in our body language and other non-verbal communication. Instead, try to stay calm, make eye contact and smile. Let your confidence shine.

Clarify

Show an interest in the people you talk to. Ask questions and seek clarification on any points that could be easily misunderstood.

Be Positive

Try to remain positive and cheerful. People are much more likely to be drawn to you if you can maintain a positive attitude.

Empathize

Understand that other people may have different points of view. Try to see things from their perspective. You may learn something while gaining the respect and trust of others.

Understand Stress

Learn to recognize, manage and reduce stress in yourself and others. Although stress is not always bad, it can have a detrimental effect on your interpersonal communication. Learning how to recognize and manage stress, in yourself and others, is an important personal skill.

Learn to be Assertive

You should aim to be neither passive nor aggressive. Being assertive is about expressing your feelings and beliefs in a way that others can understand and respect. Assertiveness is fundamental to successful negotiation.

Reflect and Improve

Think about previous conversations and other interpersonal interactions; learn from your mistakes and successes. Always keep a positive attitude but realize that we can always improve our communication skills.

Negotiate

Learn how to effectively negotiate with others paving the way to mutual respect, trust and lasting interpersonal relations.

Working in Groups

We often find ourselves in group situations, professionally and socially. Learn all about the different types of groups and teams.

Ways to Be Job and Work Skills Smart

Work is labor for pay. Employers hire you to perform skills. To maximize your power and value in the workplace, it is vital that you,

Know what skills are.

Know the different types of skills.

Make your list of skills.

Identify your Motivated Skills, Dependable Strengths.

Identify the skills employers want.

Effectively communicate your skills to employers.

Strengthen and learn new work skills.

These practical steps will help you in getting a good job, writing a resume, interviewing well, and finding careers that use similar skills. It may also open up self-employment ideas and make working for yourself a viable option.

WHAT ARE YOUR SKILLS?

Strengths

Weaknesses

Strengths	Weaknesses

S.M.A.R.T. Goal Questionnaire

SHORT TERM (9 – 12 MONTHS)

NAME:_____ DATE:_____

1. Specific- What do you want to accomplish? Is it well-defined and is the outcome clear?

_____

_____

_____

2. Measurable- How will you measure whether or not the goal has been reached (list at least two ways)?

_____

_____

_____

3. Achievable- Is it possible? Have others done it successfully? Do you have the necessary knowledge, skills, abilities, and resources to accomplish the goal? Will meeting the goal challenge you without defeating you?

_____

_____

_____

4. Relevant- What is the reason, purpose, or benefit of accomplishing the goal? What is the result (not activities leading up to the result) of the goal?

_____

_____

_____

5. Timely- What is the completion date and does that completion date create a practical sense of urgency?

_____

_____

_____

S.M.A.R.T. Goal Questionnaire
LONG TERM (2 - 4 YEARS)

NAME:_____ DATE:_____

1. Specific- What do you want to accomplish? Is it well-defined and is the outcome clear?

_____

_____

_____

2. Measurable- How will you measure whether or not the goal has been reached (list at least two ways)?

_____

_____

_____

3. Achievable- Is it possible? Have others done it successfully? Do you have the necessary knowledge, skills, abilities, and resources to accomplish the goal? Will meeting the goal challenge you without defeating you?

_____

_____

_____

4. Relevant- What is the reason, purpose, or benefit of accomplishing the goal? What is the result (not activities leading up to the result) of the goal?

_____

_____

_____

5. Timely- What is the completion date and does that completion date create a practical sense of urgency?

_____

_____

_____

Chapter Five

Bringing it all Together

REVIEW AND DISCUSSION

WHAT DID YOU LEARN.....

About Substance Abuse and Chemical Dependency

About Making Good Decisions

About Managing Your Anger

About Conflict Resolution

About Attitude

About Behaviors

About Problem Solving

About Setting Goals

Know your Strengths and Weaknesses

Know Your Skills

KNOW YOUR WORTH!

YOU CAN HAVE
RESULTS
- OR -
EXCUSES
NOT BOTH.

Complete Questionnaire to obtain a Certificate

Print Name_____

Age_____

Why are you taking this course?

_____

_____

Answer the following questions

1. How do you perceive people who abuse drugs?

2. How common is drug abuse among youth in your community?

3. Why do you think some young people abuse drugs?

4. What could cause young people to experiment with alcohol, tobacco, the non-medical use of prescription drugs or illegal drugs in the first place?

5. Is drug abuse considered normal behavior?

6. What are the living conditions of people who abuse drugs regularly?

7. How does a lifestyle involving drug abuse differ from how you want to live your life?

8. What do you think vulnerability means in terms of drug abuse?

9. What are the factors that place some people more at risk of becoming dependent on drugs than others?

10. What are the short and long term physical effects of drug abuse?

11. What are the impacts of drug abuse on the brain? Why is this so dangerous?

12. Is it safe to take drugs even if they are not considered illegal? What are the risks?

13. Why is it dangerous to take prescription drugs not prescribed by a doctor?

14. Why do some people think prescription drugs are safe even when used for non-medical purposes?

15. What kind of groups are particularly vulnerable to this kind of drug abuse?

COMPLETE THE SENTENCES

16. The Choices you make will help you get _____.

17. Your decisions will allow you to_____.

18. Anger is an _____ ranging in intensity from irritation to fury or rage.

19. One of the most effective approaches for managing anger is to _____ of the anger you experience.

20. A great way to reduce stress is to improve your _____.

21. We can manage _____ when we learn to defuse it before it becomes destructive.

22. Conflict can be avoided if steps are taken early in a discussion to diffuse anger and _____.

23. Some people believe that they have to hold their anger in to control it. This is not an effective anger _____.

24. Miscommunication contributes to frustrating _____.

25. If you're angry, it's often difficult to express yourself _____.

26. Much of your behavior depends on your _____.

27. A positive attitude can be developed by monitoring and disciplining your _____ on a moment-by-moment basis.

28. You must be willing to put energy and time to pursue _____ in order to change your mental attitude.

29. Positive thinking can lead to a lot of _____ in your life.

30. You can change your future by changing your _____.

31. Nothing is more important than how you feel and think about _____.

32. Handle mistakes and failures in a more_____ way.

33. A useful way of making goals more powerful is to use the _____ mnemonic.

34. It is important to set goals that you can _____.

35. Goals should be straightforward and _____ what you want to happen.

36. Interpersonal skills are the life skills we use every day to _____ and interact with other people, both individually and in a group.

37. Listening is not the same as _____.

38. People are much more likely to be drawn to you if you can maintain

    _____.

39. You can have results or _____ not both.

40. Identify 5 of your weaknesses.

    1.

    2.

    3.

    4.

    5.

41. Identify 5 of your strengths.

    1.

    2.

    3.

    4.

    5.

42. Write 3 short term goals.

    1.

    2.

    3.

43. Write 3 long term goals.

    1.

    2.

    3.

44. What did you learn from this course?

To receive a Certificate upon completion, send us a copy of the completed test with all of your information and mailing address.

The Streets Don't Love You Back Movement

P.O. Box 1093

Maricopa, Arizona 85139

For more information about us

Visit us at:

www.thestreetsdontloveyouback.com

BOYD AND LUCINDA RADIO SHOW

Real People... Real Stories... Real Changes...
Join us as we hear the truth about
Gangs, Drugs, Violence, Abuse
and other Life Issues.

LIVE EVERY WEDNESDAY NIGHT
8:30 PM PT/9:30 MT/10:30 CT/11:30 ET

347-826-7273

THE STREETS DON'T LOVE YOU BACK

Subscribe with iTunes

Live ON AIR

NOTES

NOTES

NOTES